Oblivion

Disguised

Joe Walsh

Inherit The Earth

Modern Classics

OBLIVION DISGUISED

By

JOE WALSH

ISBN: 9798372812697

Words Joe Walsh ©2023

Original photograph Elgin Railway Station in 1975
– Kate Walsh ©1975/2023

Additional front cover artwork/design - Meek ©2023

First edition published by

Inherit The Earth Publications

©2023

In conjunction with Amazon.

Edited

By

CT Meek

Preface

This is Joe's second published book, his first being *Joe A.k.a.* His second edition, *Oblivion Disguised*, is a masterpiece in confessional literature, an honest appraisal of his life and relationships, and his struggles against social alienation. He delves deep into his raw psyche to produce a lyrical, unmolested written truth as he's lived it, and has been generous in his openness to the reader. This offering has been carefully crafted and bookended with two wonderful, brutally honest compositions of two people close to him. Joe has left himself at the mercy of his reader, as all true artists should.

CT Meek
2023

For
Paddy, Rubie, Lady, Judy, Wee Gyp, Big Gyp.

Contents

[1]

Done (Her)

I could see the change in her gradually, steadily, as she got older. It didn't creep up on her stealthily, as I had expected. Instead it rushed at her openly, like a lioness rushing a zebra, and took hold of her while we spectated. He said she was a cave mother and didn't want to let us go. So once she didn't feel so needed anymore, as a mother, it was game over. I mean, once we started to disagree and ignore her advice. Advice that often felt more like restraints.

She didn't like letting go. I mean it must have been easier for her before, when we were still small. I am sure it was fear of us being hurt or lost, that made her need to have control. I mean, you have to have control of children right? Or else anything could happen at any time. I realise there had to be systems, procedures, guidelines, otherwise how would thirteen people in a three bedroom house ever be organised. But when do guidelines become rules?

She could feed us all on thin air, so it seemed. And keep us warm and clean. It's a mystery to me still. The scraps of paper and backs of envelopes, covered in hopeful sums, adding, subtracting, like desperate swotting for some arithmetic exam. Making friends with Peter and Paul, currying favour to pay for it all. The endless financial balancing act, she should have been an accountant.

Some began to leave, the older ones, who went laughing and dancing, finding freedom from rules that had started to bend and stretch. The same rules that she had once stretched. The natural order and vanguard I suppose, after those first small expeditions in to the adult world. Latched on to by others also feeling their way, excited and eager to make good their escape. The rules accepted those early escapes, the numbers were still on her side in the early days.

Old style rat-catchers never put their hand in the sack to pull out the last two or three. That's when they got bitten, trapped rats cannot flee. There is safety in numbers, less chance of being seen, of being caught and of being the sacrificial lamb. In reverse, attention is focussed from the many on to the few. Concentrated, suffocating, disabling, undermining, co-dependent, oppressive love. A velvet trap, but still a trap.

The change saw her strength and resilience dwindle and her personality shrivel. From big, fierce and strong, to scared and small. Diminished. It didn't take long. Frighteningly quick in fact, to reduce and shrink. So that in the morgue I said she wasn't my mother. But the others knew. The others knew better and grieved and suffered. I stood outside and felt myself fall into anger and pain while I cried and hugged a wall.

He saw the change more than any of us. He felt it more because he was still rejected. Second fiddle to his children for years and no more wanted when they were nowhere near. 'If I could get this ring off my finger!' she lamented and threatened countless times. I didn't realise then that she was done with it, and meant it, and he never let the idea enter his mind. I made sure her wish came true and had it removed. When I placed it on his palm, he closed his hand tight along with his eyes.

First I Was, Then I Was

At first I was quite empty,
As a balloon or a ball.
Then I began to fill myself,
As I learned of potentials.

And I learned how to be free!
I was a galleon on the sea,
Braving tempest gales,
At bath-time on Sundays.

Then I was wild and wary,
A mustang on the prairie,
Or a sleek mountain lion,
Roaming free in our living room.

Barefit Broth

She said,
Run a message tae the shoaps,
An hurry back, dinnae git loast,
Here's a shillin', mind hud it tight,
Get a pound o' ingens wi it.

Run aw the wey thair, an walk straight back,
Dinnae lose the change an dinnae droap the bag,
Here's hopin' the meter winnae need the shillin',
But it's a choice atween light, or soup withoot ingens.

That must huv been the last siller boab,
If it wis only ingens fir Barefit Broth.
Nae fit tea fir a man's been labourin' aw week,
No even wi saut and pepper and thick buttered breid.

She could rob Peter tae pey Paul wi the best o thum,
And go bare legged, an walk tall wi the rest o thum,
But some night's thir wis less want an mair need,
An it jist hud tae be Barefit Broth an breid.

The Hare

Faither ah tried hard tae please ye,
But human frailty oft did trip me.
When ah broucht hame mah trophy tae ye,
Ah saw yir condemnation o me.
Disapproval on yir face,
Fir the murder o nature's grace.
Mother an bairns in a scullery basin,
Aw fir the sake o a faither's praisin'.

What part o the lesson did ah ignore?
Fae verse ah read, sae hert-felt wrote,
Thit tae hurt a creature wid be loath,
An innocent traiveller on life's road.
Faither ah can see yir face on that day,
Set and stern ahind yir paper,
Contemplating how ah managed,
Tae cairry oot sich brutal action.

An then the quest fir how ah achieved,
Wi only bare hands an a dug wi little speed,
The body o a creature extinguished fae life,
Fir nae reason other thin a youth's braggin' rights.
An yince strode hame wi the show o mah prowess,
The demand tae examine how the corpse ah possessed,
Could hae gi'en up living wi sae little reason,
Tae a laddie an a stane an his deadly ambition.

O Faither yir face haunts me tae this later day,
Even though noo mah confession is made.
The weicht in mah sowl remains hard and heavy,
Tae be mah reminder, as well as the levy,
Tae regard nature's seasons as they pass through the landscape,
An pey due respect tae the clues thit they leave thair.
Ah dinnae ask forgiveness, ah stand only wi humility,
Tae yir memory ah wish only tae bare mah humanity.

[6]

Sae long backwards noo, ah cast my thouchts,
Lang syne the day thit lent me conscience,
An has troubled me since, awake and in dream,
An gnawed at the sense o mah ain self-belief.
Faither, though that we cannae see forads,
We can task thit oor wisdom improves wi age,
But as a poet said yince o the best laid schemes,
As o mice and men, they gang aft agley.

Doon Thair Fir Dancin'

Up here fir thinkin', doon thair fir dancin' son, ei said,
An dinnae talk tae me aboot that gay thing,
Because ah dinnae understand it.
Ah took that oan the chin an the love ei could gie.

Ah gote a joab in the Sighthill Inn dad, ah said,
Well keep yir fingers oot the Till son, ei said.
But it's a poor barman cannae make fags an a pint oan shift eh!
Up here fir thinkin', doon thair fir dancin' dad, ah said,
An dinnae talk tae me aboot fitbaw,
Because ah dinnae understand it.
Ei took that oan the chin an the love ah could gie.

Up here fir thinkin', doon thair fir dancin' son, ei said,
Though ei didnae take his ain advice aw the time did ei!
Ei wis only human and whae gote it right ivery time eh?
No you and no me! Facts are chiels thit winna ding Burns said,
Nae man is perfect, an a man's a man fir aw that eh!

Mah auld man said, dinnae make mountains oot o moles holes!
Ye can take a hoarse tae water but ye canny make it jump in!
Live yir life!
Get an education!
Up here fir thinkin', doon thair fir dancin' son!

[8]

Those Feelings

When I felt that way,
Isolated, ashamed,
Detestable and angry,
My words were razor blades.

My tongue made words to self-justify,
My eyes looked out from my disguise,
And masked where they stopped,
To contemplate little bottles.

Green

I lived between the devil and the deep blue sea. I didn't know, between the two half's of me, who I should be. The wind of change stroked my face while unseen urges pulled me in opposite ways. The urges were strong, tidal, currents that consumed and swept all along.

Adventure! Young men need adventure, and excitement. Young men are built and designed to have it. Driven by desire and testosterone, reckless and not bullet-shy at all. Yet, so fragile, with hidden fears and thoughts, and vulnerable to the slipping knot.

Like lunar tide again the urges came, in waves, where should this young man find his relief? Hidden in normality? Where difference is weakness and plain to see, unless you can hide it, make it unseen, and live the lie that suffocates your mind.

I loved green and light. All the different greens of the countryside. Has anyone counted the many different shades I wondered, as I lay amongst it, or waded through it, or looked up through it, and dreamed of making love in it.

The grey and honey coloured sandstone, and the ingrained sooty black of the town had its own austere beauty and allure. It tempted and beckoned and offered and bribed and Oh, how it lured. Splashes of green peek-a-booed amongst the black, and honey and grey. Green that waved and said hello to me, shyly.

The town was a mongrel bitch, available to all and satisfied an itch. It was dangerous, and conniving, a con-artist and used to surviving on its lies and wit. It was a maze, a conundrum; it made promises it instantly forgot and abandoned like kittens in an oil drum.

The town was harsh, always bustle and crush, people deafened, blinkered, in their rush. What made beggars with nowhere to live, think that one day they would be noticed or given sympathy? And what difference would one new boy make to the daily grind?

[10]

It took so long to learn. But it always takes an unwilling mind longer to learn, and some never do. Some never leave, not of their own free will, or intentionally. You can get used to grime, and pain, and disdain after a time. Until it becomes a way of life, like prison.

So the trick is to not get settled, and to not forget what you had before, and what you wanted years ago. I loved green. The green of the leaves high up in the trees, and I liked to be clean. Clean and fresh as the air under a falcons wing, as oxygenating as a crystal spring.

Tides come in and tides go out. Minds change and so do doubts, into certainty. Mists lift, sands shift and become concrete level. I learned to learn, and listen to the urges as they came and agreed to be tamed, like wild horses.

Neath Summer Moon Once In Youth

Neath summer moon once in our youth,
Our love was urgent and our love was sure,
In that secret place hidden in sweet meadow,
Our passion and caresses were true joy to know.

Hidden through gloaming time and the short night,
Too soon ending loves dream, with its bustle and light,
Hasty morning, urging the city back to life,
Love to be hidden again and denied.

Life then was a song joyously learned and sung,
A song composed only for the courage of the young,
We couldn't know it would be over too soon,
But that didn't matter neath the silver summer moon.

Fish Eyes

He feels dead inside,
He sees the world through fish eyes.

He spits empty words,
Spilled from heart numb.

He doesn't want to be alive,
Fuck this genetic code to survive!

Look into his gaze,
And feel his cold daze.

He feels dead inside,
And looks through fish eyes.

Trade

There were shadows in the shadows,
In the park after dark,
Drifting shapes haunted the gates,
And lowered voices made choices.

While the city slept,
Deals were made and promises kept,
Secrets traded,
Quietly, as lust gave way,
To guilt, fear and shame.

Quiet footsteps in the starlight,
Sure-footed undercover of night,
Led to hushed rustling,
From rushed fumbling.

By a tree a lighter blazed,
A glimpse of a face,
Then warm tempting haze,
As he sucked in smoke,
From the red burning glow,
Only to further his aim,
And draw the moth to the flame.

And you froze before you melted,
And laid your soul bare,
Then struck a match to return the flare,
And drew the smoke in deep,
As you leaned back against your tree,
And wondered why you did it,
While you died a little.

The Drip That Breaks The Stone

Are you running out of time?
Have you been waiting very long?
Will your patience keep aligned?
With the drip that breaks the stone.
The clock hands' tireless tick,
Tiny steps towards your goal,
And the rhythm of your heartbeat,
Are of the drip that breaks the stone.

Is time the drip that breaks the stone?
Over lifetimes', not ours alone.
The wearing down of soul and bone,
Relentless, is the drip that breaks the stone!
The ache of life upon your back,
Bent and resigned to carry on,
With the slog of living in this world,
A life-time of drips that break the stone.

Are you the drip that breaks the stone?
You who grind the wheels of work and love,
The one who daily jeers and taunts,
The helpless, powerless and torn.
Cruel are the minds who serve their own,
Twisted souls who bad use power,
Icy hearts thaw toxic streams,
And bitter drips that break the stone.

Does your heart yearn to be released?
From the yoke of time's own tyranny,
From days enslaved to being freed,
Loosed into breathless tranquillity.
Do you dream of an empty horizon?
As you countdown towards oblivion,
Will you embrace longed for extinction?
As the last drip falls and breaks the stone.

Soldier On

I marched on, I marched on,
And my boots they pounded and they pounded.
I looked up, I looked all around,
But all I saw was sky and ground.
I did not see the moon afar,
Or sun eclipsed, or tumbling stars,
I looked up and all around,
But all I saw was sky and ground.

I tramped on, across the world,
It seemed so full and then so empty.
I looked around, I looked around,
But all I saw was sky and ground.
I did not see noble forest arches,
Felled and burned and turned to ashes,
I looked around, I looked around,
But all I saw was sky and ground.

I trudged on, I trudged on,
The world was full of new excitement.
I went in search, I went in seek,
But always it was out of reach.
I reached with hands not meant to feel,
My eyes were wide but did not see,
I went in search, I went in seek,
But always joy was out of reach.

I plodded on, I plodded on,
And the chances came and then were gone.
I held on, I held on, and,
All I held was trickling sand.
The cards I turned always against me,
The dice I rolled gave no favour to me,
I held on, I held on, and,
All I held was trickling sand.

[16]

Soldier on, Soldier on,
The life I lead has been a lone journey.
Join me, come along with me,
To explore the stars and galaxy.
I march on, and march on,
My boots will pound and they will pound.
Walk with me some of the way,
My life has been a lone journey.

Just Left Alone

We wanted just to be left alone, mostly. Left alone and not noticed, generally. So that we could live our lives and find some recognition and acceptance from our peers mainly. Who were the only ones who understood completely, and who got the jokes and off-the-cuff remarks totally! Left alone so that we could get from A to B without abuse or attack, and maybe even also get safely back.

Mostly we just wanted to be ignored, or not seen, and definitely not heard. But that was not always possible, when we had no control over the inevitable; raids by the police on our little clubs and pubs by six foot plus men built like brick shit-houses. Many of who were actual six foot plus shite-houses, who forced into our flats to threaten us in our privately owned spaces, or laughed as they watched the queer bashers punch our pretty faces.

We wanted it to stop and to be left alone. It was hard enough being an embarrassment and disowned, by those that said they loved us from before we were even born. Love can clearly be conditional if it prevents the confrontational from demanding the exceptional; and acceptance without disclaimers to excuse the unacceptable.

Now you say we are to stop, Mr Clever-Clogs! Just for a month though, during the World Cup. Tell us oh so cleverly then, have the Catholics to stop being Catholics during the Orange-men's parades? Can you cleverly stop being black yourself if you think we can stop being gay? Why would you support the tournament in Qatar at all? If equality, and beating modern slavery meant more to you, than for instance gas, oil, or a ball. So can you drop your shameless front and just stop; pretending you're not a cunt.

Mostly we wanted to be just left alone, but that has forever changed. We survived, well most of us anyway, the violence, the hate fuelled laws, and our families estranged. The next generations have demanded more, much more, than just to be left alone. The closet doors have been well and truly blown, silenced voices and shrinking violets retreat in shame no more.

[18]

The Kindness Of Strangers

Beware the kindness of strangers,
It may disguise dark and bloody dangers,
On accepting the hand of benevolence,
You may enter a contract of malevolence.

The kindness of strangers can feel real,
But may be false and superficial,
Remember nothing much is free,
And friendship may come with a fee.
Tenderness, maybe,
Happiness, could be,
Temporary!
A lie for a lie,
A truth for a truth.

In smiling company,
Especially,
Beware the hidden danger,
Within the kindness of strangers!

Threats

They will be at your door soon,
Very soon,
The young girl's voice whined,
Tinny, common, out of tune.

I knew who she was,
That took her by surprise,
And scared her,
Her tinny whining tailed off,
When I asked how her brother was,
And she hung up.

I still slept with a three foot length,
Of curtain-pole under the bed,
In easy reach,
Because you never knew,
With those crazy fuckers.

It's hard to act like normal,
And go to work,
Scared to leave the flat,
Scared to stay in it,
It's a real dilemma.

The phone calls through the night,
All night!
Stranger's unattached voices,
Threatening violence,
Making indecent propositions.

Threats, abuse, from who?
That is the scary bit,
Wondering, who is watching you!

Life in a cloud,
Dark and oppressive all around,

An atmosphere of suspicion and doubt,
All that hate,
So heavy I thought I would suffocate.

The Windae

She wis hingin' oot the windae,
Moanin' somethin' quietly,
Leanin' ower the windae ledge,
Hur airms hingin',
Jist hingin'.

She wis shoutin' fir me thair,
She said, when ah foond hur,
Half leanin', half hingin,
Hur heid oan hur airm.

"Ah wis shoutin' fir ye,
Ye wir due hame," she said.
Ah helped hur reach,
Ower tae the settee,
An she lay doon,
An passed oot.

If ah hudnae been skivin' the school,
Ah widdah been ten minutes sooner.

Let There Be Love

Everyone has their own way of giving,
Everyone has their own way of living,
Everyone comes, everyone goes,
Everyone everywhere, we all come and go.
Everyone comes from their own direction,
Everyone goes to their own destination,
Look at us come, watch us all go,
Everyone everywhere, we all come and go.

But let there be love,
Let there be love,
Cosmic Lennon Love,
Let there be love.

Everyone reaches their own conclusion,
Everyone hides behind their own illusion,
Look at us hide, look at us seek,
Everyone everywhere, we all hide and seek.
Everyone comes in their own small footsteps,
Everyone leaves in their own unique foot prints,
Everyone comes, everyone leaves,
Everyone everywhere, we all come and leave.

But let there be love,
Let there be love,
Cosmic Lennon Love,
Let there be love.

Everyone forms their very own impression,
Everyone makes their own interpretation,
Look at us learn, look at us grow,
Everyone everywhere should all learn and grow.
Everyone starts in their very own story,
Everyone ends when the last page closes,
Everyone starts, everyone ends,
Everyone everywhere, we all start and end.

But let there be love,
Let there be love,
All we need is love, love!
Cosmic Lennon love,
Let there be love.

Tumble

I heard the door bang,
Like a cannon,
I felt my heart tumble,
Over and over,
I felt your voice hit me,
Like a hammer,
I felt my heart tumble,
Over and over.

I can't breathe,
I can't think,
I can't sleep.

Come back,
Don't leave,
Stay here.

I heard the door bang,
Like a cannon,
I felt my heart tumble,
Over and over,
I felt your voice hit me,
Like a hammer,
I felt my heart tumble,
Over and over.

Her Pillow

All that she left was her imprint,
In the pillow,
And her smell,
Still alive.

The deep imprint of her head,
In white, pink and mauve floral.
I still have the duvet set,
From her bed,
In a cupboard somewhere,
Laundered and folded.
I didn't mean to hang on to it,
Someone could use it.

The round, deep imprint of her head,
In the pillow,
Was all that she left,
And my head fitted perfectly,
Where it had waited for hours,
After the ambulance took her away.

They pulled me from the bed,
I don't know why I let them,
Or why they couldn't let me,
Bury my face there in grief.
I returned after,
To sit there again,
But it was too late,
It wasn't the same.

The Last Thing

It's the last thing you did wrong that damns you!
It doesn't matter what went before,
All the times you put someone before you,
And all the things they thanked you for.

Beware those bad days when you are scared,
Those times when you weren't quite right,
Under the weather, nerves frayed,
On your own, lonely, feeling small in the dark night.

And you make a poor decision,
You do something you normally wouldn't,
And all the good things you said and did,
Are forgotten in a red mist instant.

The flames of anger are fiercely fanned,
Your fingers are burned,
On both of your hands,
And that last thing has you damned!

Travelling Tradition

Travelling tradition, live to be free,
My hearts with the horse folk,
Itchy feet.
Travelling tradition, nowhere to be,
My hearts with the horse folk.
Travelling, travelling,
Oh, to be,
Travelling, travelling,
With all my cares behind me.

Towards the horizon, never quite reaching,
Always far in the distance,
Never arriving.
Towards the horizon, no reason for striving,
Always far in the distance.
Travelling, travelling,
Oh, to be,
Travelling, travelling,
With all my cares behind me.

The sense of freedom, when no one is waiting,
And no one to promise,
No explaining.
Such a sense of freedom, when no one is waiting,
And no one to promise.
Travelling, travelling,
Oh, to be,
Travelling, travelling,
With all my cares behind me.

Travelling tradition, live to be free,
My hearts with the horse folk,
Itchy feet.
Travelling tradition, nowhere to be,
My hearts with the horse folk.

[28]

Travelling, travelling,
Oh, to be,
Travelling, travelling,
With all my cares behind me.

Oblivion Disguised

Where will you run to now Joe?
Where will you hide away?
What stormy dreams are you packing up,
And taking with you on your way?

Who are you going to turn to Joe,
Now that your friends are ghosts?
The sacrificial lamb is bones,
And love has turned to stone.

Where will you run to now Joe?
Where are you going to go?
When the smoke clears the mirror,
And the universe unfolds.

Mistaken for eternity, here lies the golden truth,
Oblivion disguised for the eyes of mortal youth.
And now the youth is a man Joe,
Look! The truth has been exposed,
Where will you run to now Joe?
Where are you going to go?

The Dance

I saw an eclipse of the sun, I saw a man walk on the moon,
I saw the face of a baby, light up a room.

I saw a caterpillar become a moth, and a tadpole become a frog, I
saw the sun set behind a mountain, and the moon rise through the
fog.

I saw an avalanche and a landslide, I saw a sandstorm and tidal
wave, I saw an ocean storm in winter, and the hillside shelter a hare.

I saw shooting stars in the evening, and meteors in the morning, I
saw children in armies toting rifles and wearing uniforms.

I saw women and men enslaved, I saw babies washed up on beaches,
I saw their mothers in the waves, and their fathers in despair.

I saw men, women, and children dig with bare hands in to rubble, as
they listened for cries from the souls buried under.

I saw rockets go into space, I saw machines dive into oceans, I saw a
man run a world record, and another man live his dream.

I saw saints help the homeless, I saw angels on the pavement, I saw
a young girl demand justice, many listened to her.

I saw insects like jewels, and fireworks that entranced, I saw birds
that bedazzled, and I saw the smiling gypsy dance.

Yes, I saw the smiling gypsy dance.

Big Brother

You finally had your way,
You just had to stick to your story,
Or more to the point,
Deny what you said.

It's the spaces between the words,
That gives you away.
The silences,
The gaps between sentences,
And the looks.
Or more to the point,
When you look away,
To shield your eyes,
From what they might recognise,
Or let slip.

And the drumming of your fingers,
On the worn leather of the chair,
Worried thin by those same guilty fingers,
Over decades.

Because it's a very old chair,
But not as old as the memory,
That you are determined not to share,
Because that would be testimony,
To your crime,
Against me.

You are way more oppressed than me.
Oh, the crushing pressure of guilt felt by the guilty!
Embarrassed, scared and ashamed,
Of what might be discovered.

I am glad I had the balls,
To live through it all and reject,
Those roles and duties so expected.

[32]

Don't worry,
I think you got away with it,
No-one now will penetrate,
The depth and the layers,
Of your disguise.

You live with your betrayal,
But it poisons you daily,
I see its shadow unlike the others.

I am trapped by devotion,
But I don't forgive you,
Big Brother.

Little Big-Man

I didn't mean to hurt you,
You just got in the way,
Of my anger and my pain.

If I could rewind,
Just to that night,
I would change it.

We were young men,
Both hurting then,
In our own pain.

The thing that haunts my mind,
Was that I knew of yours,
But you couldn't know of mine.

I'm sorry I hurt you,
I let you get in the way,
Of my anger and my pain.

Picardy Place

It was good to meet and sit on the sunny street with a beer,
You chose a good part of town for the sun to be on our backs.
The lager was tasteless and too expensive, did you think so as well?

But I am so out of touch,
With the city and the gay places,
What would I know?
When did they make Edinburgh into a shameless hustler?

The traffic was non-stop,
Although I never heard it much,
Humming city machine in the background.
Passers-by were friendly and inquisitive,
So multi-cultural and intercontinental.
I liked the feel and the buzz of it all.

A car went through a red light at the nearby junction,
You told me about it, my back was towards it.
I told you about my brush with death at the same place,
That was forty years before.
Neither of us thought it was remarkable or said any more.
Is that to be blasé, or cool, or in denial?

The young man we spoke to left me with a sad impression,
He reminded me of someone I used to know.
Same mannerisms, same accent, and same forced joviality.

He wore multiple rings on his fingers,
Like the Old-Town-Edinburgh women of previous generations,
Wearing their wealth and status on their fingers and in their ears.

Like Tom's mother, Julia,
From Edinburgh Cowgate,
Who had nothing but what she stood up in.

[35]

Three fingers of gold rings,
And torn ear-lobes,
Nowhere for her long ago hawked half sovereigns.

The young man was still good looking and youthful at a first glance,
But he looked slightly jaded and clouds passed across his face.
His skin was tight from the sun and party lifestyle in Benidorm,
And he was half-drunk from the lunchtime cocktails at £12 a pop.
An early start to the Friday night out!

He gave too much away when he laughed, and,
Made off the cuff remarks.
He smiled as if he was happy but his eyes had a distant misty look,
And he was desperate to be told he looked younger than he was.
I think it was Tom he reminded me of before he gave in.

Island Life

Island life, I kinda' got used to this island life,
To being here on my own in my stranded life,
In this human ocean, searching the skyline,
In this island life, my island life.

And I feel like Robinson Crusoe on a Saturday night,
With my own company in my island life,
And I could give up hope but I know I still have time,
So I keep wishing and hoping and keep my dream alive.

Island life, you know it's not all bad in my island life,
Visitors reach my shore sometimes and see me right,
But then leave me castaway in this sea of life,
In this island life, my island life.

And I feel like Robinson Crusoe on a Saturday night,
With my own company in my island life,
And I could give up hope but I know I still have time,
So I keep wishing and hoping and keep my dream alive.

Island life, when was I washed up into this island life?
I didn't see this happen in my drifting life,
Then I woke on my desert island and looked back through time,
At this island life, my island life.

And I feel like Robinson Crusoe on a Saturday night,
With my own company in my island life,
And I could give up hope but I know I still have time,
So I keep wishing and hoping and keep my dream alive.

Island life, I kinda' got used to this island life,
To being here on my own in my stranded life,
In this human ocean, searching the skyline,
In this island life, my island life.

And I feel like Robinson Crusoe on a Saturday night,
With my own company in my island life,
And I could give up hope but I know I still have time,
So I keep wishing and hoping and keep my dream alive.

No-Man's Land

Once I stood where the rainbow lands,
And rode a prancing unicorn,
Along a Celtic strand,
Once.

And once, a young man ridiculed an old man's reveries,
Now the young man lives in an old man's memories.
He wanted to dance and sing, to love and to roam,
Forever be strong and brave with no need of home.

Where is the line drawn in shifting sand?
The fine-line that is a subtle command!
The line that can be a knife edge,
The water's edge,
Or a cliff edge.

The sun-dial marks time silently, like rain drops down a pane,
While the sand in the hour-glass marks it grain by grain.
Do the raindrops scream on their way down the glass?
And do the grains of sand thunder as they collide and crash?

Where is my home?
I want to be there,
But my home is nowhere,
And yet everywhere.

It's where I stand,
And here where I am,
In no-man's land.

What O Loss?

Its wi heavy hert the day,
Ah sit an think o you and me,
An ponder if bonds tae faimily,
Are as gossamer in thair fragility.
Though that was not ay how they wir,
First forged fae love wi fearsome care,
Within a hame that wis maist blessed,
Wi kinship strength thit knew nae rest.

What wir yince o steel an bonded ticht,
Attachments close an fused wi micht,
Years o life hae undermined,
An noo fail tae pass the test o time.
The ties o faimily come loose an faw,
The race tae be near slows tae a crawl,
Sibling bonds become as prison chains,
When freedom or love caws oor name.

Ah surely though will niver understand,
What ah did sae coorse, sae underhand,
Thit made ye want tae take against me,
An cast a stane at mah company.
Ah dout thit we or many ithers,
Hae conscience thit is snaw-white brither,
Ah see ye turn yir back wi ease,
But no sae smairtly the ither cheek.

So here ah sit in solemn reflection,
At pains tae make sense o this dissection,
It seems wilfu' waste tae lose the trust,
O a brither yince close, but lose if ye must.
The real dinger though is eftir aw these years,
Thir seems sae little worthy o tears,
Tae mah surprise, but wi nae relief,
Ah find little left tae miss or grieve.

[40]

So what o loss, an hurt an pain?
Ah find thaim absent here the day,
If ah had sense o regret or remorse,
Ah wid feel ah've loast something o human worth.
It's the thing that rankles or causes pain,
Thit's better awa an left alane.
The gift we hae o bein a brither,
Is tae ken we hae nae debt tae each ither.

Vulture

Dear brother,
I know you struggle with my dislike of your friend,
It may then help you to read this note to the end.

He is a scavenger, a cadger, a scrounger, a vulture,
He is a tapper and a specimen of life's lower order.
With smugness he guzzled the last beer of a grieving man,
And came back the next day to drain the dregs from empty cans.

The grieving man was our father, weakened and beaten low,
Off his guard, the good host, conned by the guiser at his door.
No, he will never be welcome on my shore,
And he would be unwise to ever darken my door.

You are his friend,
Though I fail to comprehend.
Perhaps he may be yours,
Or else his means to an end.

Sincerely,
Joe.

Who Gets The Blame?

Who gets the blame?
And the shame,
When the game is played out again,
Because you know,
It always ends this way.

What happened to the choices?
From all the men you knew,
And the houses of cards,
Where dreams didn't come true.

Your dark glasses are no use in the gloom,
Of the moon-glow in your rented room,
For red rimmed eyes and bruised skin,
Given by the enemy that was within.

The tender demands gradually less tender,
Love bite, or bite sized bruise?
Who got to choose?
And who had to lose, again.
Who gets the blame?
And the shame?

Continental Shift

They sometimes just appear!
Sudden fractures,
That split and crack,
Creating factions,
And islands.

A continent united,
Moves on its foundations,
And finds differences,
That divide.

The parts separate,
They drift apart,
The fractures open wider,
The parts shift and become,
Distant shores,
And make strangers,
Of those once loved and close.

Wake To Dream

Good morning brother, it's been a long time,
I know your face well, do you remember mine?
There's so much I don't know yet, and I feel scared,
I've not got going yet, I still dream and dare.
So much I have seen and I have hardly begun,
And at our age, most of our living is done.
But if there was one more fight?
A new adventure, a night to excite.

Oh, one last stramash, to enjoy some violence,
The chance to be passionate, fierce and ferocious.
To be defiant, insubordinate and unmanageable,
Belligerent, non-conformist and so very oppositional.
And to feel the strength and the power of internal rebellion,
As it spills into reality, bruising ego, skin and bone.
A Clockwork Orange housing-scheme mentality,
Anger and viciousness dressed up in cool style.

Civil disobedience in Crombie and Stay-Prest,
Ben Sherman button collar and Prince Of Wales Check.
But who needs snazzy uniforms to express how you feel,
Work jeans and Tuff boots are all that you need.
What makes your blood boil, what makes your pulse race?
Who wants your attention and deserves you irate?
Brother, always remember my face,
Wake to dream and dream if you dare.

Done (Him)

He folded when his wife died. He didn't know how to be alive and;
Be a man without being a husband, a man without having a wife, to
be defined as something else, someone, as he saw it, so much less.
He was shocked when the man on the phone called him a widower,
he looked smaller and lessened, because he felt like his gender was
being questioned.

I mean, he had to ask me if a man can be, aye a widow! And I
explained he was a widower, a man widowed. Still our father, and
still the same man. But I don't think he could understand and he
shrunk into his chair. The one that was you know, 'your father's
chair', in the corner, so positioned to see the TV, the window, and
the front gate. Dad's chair, the protector and provider's throne, the
space that the husband and the father owned.

It must have started years before, when he was made redundant, long
before he was old. Maybe even before that, as far back as when he
left the building trade, where he had a reputation. Where his strength
and prowess were renowned, stoked with toxic masculinity,
imbedded deep within the core of his macho identity, on the sites
and in the pubs, supportive habitats for his fragile personality.

So I think it started then, because that was the first blow to his peace
of mind, when he finally decided to find a 'soft job' inside, out of
the weather. No more 'farmers tan', chilblained feet and frost-
hacked hands. He seemed happier, for a while anyway, then less
confident, unsure and angry. Resentful sometimes and always aware
of the new kings standing out in the wings, waiting their chance to
knock him down and steal his crown.

'Have you heard that song?' he asked my sister, 'about the man in
the corner? It gets played in the pub and it's about me, he can't keep
up, just like me.' He really knew it then, when he lost his manly
religion and felt he was lagging behind. Like the day when he
stopped with his brother to catch their breath and the park attendant
called them pervs, for being near the wee tot's play area. The

[46]

mindless cunt had no inkling of the hammer blow that was to a listing boat already sinking.

But he didn't just roll over and give in. He was never cooperative with the forces against him. I don't know if he was courageous or just awkward, bloody-minded, audacious. I don't know how I preferred him, as a vulnerable widower or as a younger man with a chip on his shoulder. I still miss the man lying drunk on his back in the dahlias, one arm raised to be hauled upwards and upright, but I don't miss holding him up so he could have a piss.

I don't miss the fights over the shrinking redundancy balance either, or the instruction not to talk to him about my sexuality. But I miss the long talks about his music and politics, of Paul Robson and Ella Fitzgerald, and playing him my latest Lou Reed to undermine his barely latent prejudices. Really it was so easy to excite a man who just wanted to be young again and to sing, dance and rebel. To enjoy the revelations that passed him by and fed the groovy generation. But I didn't know that until I was no longer young myself.

The man and his mind had been moulded by childhood poverty, war, revolution and a new world order. By sixty years old he had also survived the Thatcherite toll, but hadn't expected Blair, and Labour sold; down the river to the middle-class, or The Blues hi-jacked by the Rolling Stones. But he never survived losing his wife, he didn't know then the purpose of his life, or for his chair in the corner, and so he was done with them.

Acknowledgements

Meek: Thank you for your guidance and inspiration; Kate Walsh for the pic.

Joe
January
2023

[49]

[50]

Author

Joe Alexander Laurence Walsh
Is a retired social worker, from Edinburgh, living in Aberdeenshire
for the last 25 years. He has finally made time to write from his own
unique point of reference.

inherit_theearth@btbtinternet.com

Other work by Joe available from Amazon Books.

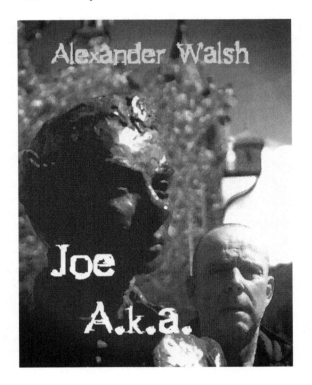

Available from Amazon
ISBN: 9798839273474

Notes

Printed in Great Britain
by Amazon

16480454R00036